Awesome, Disgusting Careers

DISGUSTING WATER AND SEWER JOBS

Mary E. Bleckwehl

BLACK RABBIT BOOKS

Hi Jinx is published by Black Rabbit Books
P.O. Box 227, Mankato, Minnesota, 56002.
www.blackrabbitbooks.com

Marysa Storm, editor; Michael Sellner, designer and photo researcher

Library of Congress Cataloging-in-Publication Data
Names: Bleckwehl, Mary Evanson, author.
Title: Disgusting water and sewer jobs / by Mary E. Bleckwehl.
Description: Mankato, Minnesota : Black Rabbit Books, [2023] | Series: Hi jinx. Awesome, disgusting careers | Includes bibliographical references and index. | Audience: Ages: 8-12 | Audience: Grades: 4-6 | Summary: "Let readers explore the awesome, disgusting water and sewer jobs that keep their world running smoothly through witty, conversational text, fun facts, and critical thinking questions that'll have them laughing and learning"- Provided by publisher.
Identifiers: LCCN 2020031322 (print) | LCCN 2020031323 (ebook) | ISBN 9781623106850 (hardcover) | ISBN 9781644665527 (paperback) | ISBN 9781623106911 (ebook)
Subjects: LCSH: Sewage disposal–Vocational guidance–Juvenile literature. | Plumbers–Juvenile literature. | Sanitation workers–Juvenile literature.
Classification: LCC HD4475 .B53 2022 (print) | LCC HD4475 (ebook) | DDC 628.1023-dc23
LC record available at https://lccn.loc.gov/2020031322
LC ebook record available at https://lccn.loc.gov/2020031323

Image Credits

123RF: Danilo Sanino, Cover, 12–13; Alamy: Bill Greenblatt, 14–15; Islandstock, 8; iStock: burdem, 16; fotolinchen, 18–19; Shutterstock: Alica in Wonderland, Cover, 16, 21; anela.k, 8; Arcady, 19; Benedek Alpar, 10; bomg, 5; Cartone Animato, 11; Hermin, 9; Jon Larter, 5; KaliAntye, 11; LoopAll, Cover, 1, 5, 6, 20; Luciano Cosmo, 2–3; Maxx-Studio, 6; Memo Angeles, Cover, 13, 20, 21; nazlisart, Cover, 12; Pasko Maksim, 23, 24; picoStudio, 18; Pitju, 21; Ratchanee Sawasdijira, 7; ridjam, 10, 11; Ripitya, 8; Ron Dale, 5, 6, 20; Stanislaw Mikulski, 7; sundatoon, Cover, 13; Thongchai Siriporn, 16; Tony Oshlick, 23; totallypic, 9, 10, 18; Vastram, 18; vetre, 16; Vladimir Mulder, 4

CONTENTS

4

Chapter 1

WORK THAT STINKS

There are many disgusting jobs needed to make the world go round. Some of the grossest are water and sewer jobs. Each one stinks! People who aren't afraid of a challenge don't mind, though. What about you? Are you brave enough to learn more?

Chapter 2

THE JOBS

Plumber

It's an emergency! Your toilet won't flush! Calling 911 won't help. But calling a plumber will. These workers can unclog smelly toilets. Sucking slime from drains is their thing. Plumbers also **install** new pipes and **fixtures**, such as sinks. They must learn building **codes** and rules. We'd be in a lot of trouble without them.

November 19th is World Toilet Day.

plugged toilet

clogged drain

PUMPING WASTE
8B3 1731

DUMPING WASTE

CLEANING SURFACES

Portable Toilet Cleaner

Some places don't have permanent bathrooms. People use portable toilets instead. When these toilets need to be cleaned, stand back! Workers use hoses to suck human waste into tanks. From the tanks, the waste goes into sewers. If a hose breaks or gets blocked, duck! We're talking flying waste! These workers also wash all the surfaces. When workers are done, there's a clean place "to go."

Septic Tank Servicer

Everything that slides down a drain needs a place to go. Some people's waste flows into **septic tanks**. These tanks are buried in their yards. Stinky sludge and scum form inside them. It's up to septic tank servicers to clean them! These workers pry the tank covers off. They push hoses through the scummy layers. The hoses suck gunk into trucks. These workers also deal with the stink to replace any worn parts.

sludge and scum

Sewer Inspector

Not everyone's waste goes into a septic tank. Most waste ends up in sewer tunnels under the streets instead. Sewer inspectors work in these tunnels. There, they inspect leaks, fix cracks in the tunnels, and break up clogs. These workers must wade and crawl through rivers of waste. They don't do this alone, though. Roaches and rats are there too. Care to join?

Hazmat Diver

A **hazmat** diver's day can mean oceans of adventure! It can also be downright disgusting. These workers swim through dangerous water. Sometimes they swim through sewage to fix pipes. They might dive into oil spills to help clean up. Protective suits and **respirators** keep them safe. Divers also get shots to prevent diseases. This isn't a job for wimps!

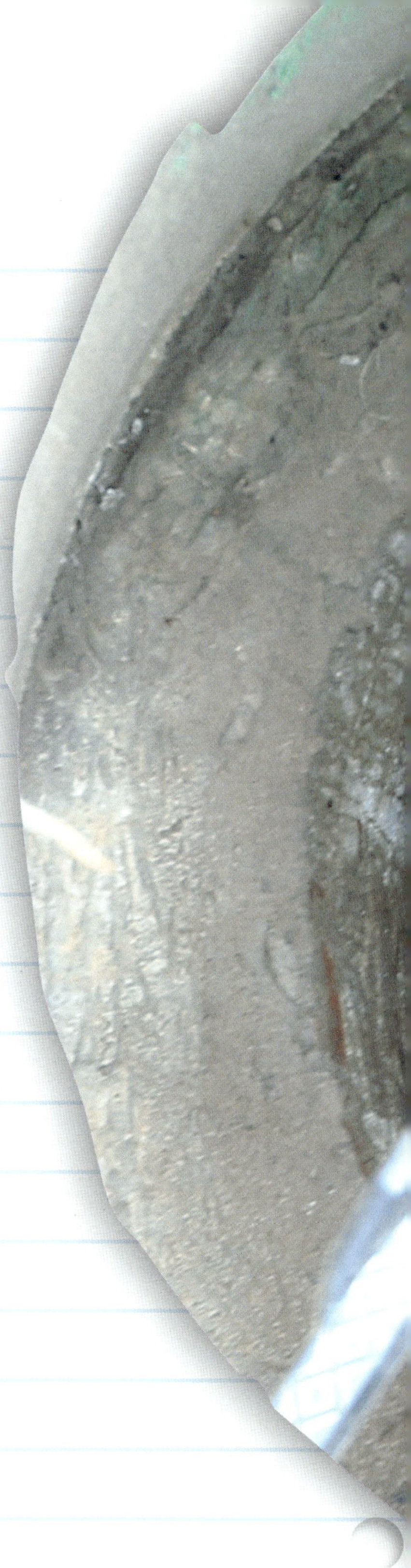

oil spill

sea turtle

cleaning garbage

Ocean Cleanup Worker

Oceans are home to colorful fish and plants. They're also full of dirty diapers, glass, and plastic bottles. It's up to cleanup crews to collect this trash. Some use nets and skimmers to scoop it up. Others wade into dark waters to clean oil spills. Some even find rotting bodies. This job is gross. But the workers make a huge difference.

A little bit of plastic can cause a lot of harm. A single piece can kill a sea turtle.

Wastewater Treatment Operator

Wastewater goes on a journey through pipes to treatment plants. There, wastewater treatment operators clean it up. They remove solid waste. Then they add **chemicals** to the dirty water. These chemicals kill **bacteria**. They make water safe to release into the environment. These workers must deal with noisy machines, slippery floors, and gross smells.

Each U.S. person produces about 100 gallons (379 liters) of wastewater a day.

Chapter 3
GET IN ON THE HI JINX

Water and sewer jobs are super important. People and animals need clean water. They need to be safe from disease. Most of these jobs require a high school diploma. People get on-the-job training too. Some workers, such as plumbers, have **apprenticeships**. Want a career that makes a difference? One of the jobs in this book might be for you.

Take It One Step More

1. What is one job in this book that you would never do? Why?

2. If you couldn't smell, would you work a sewer job?

3. Pollution is a huge problem for sea life. What can you do to help?

GLOSSARY

apprenticeship (uh-PREN-tis-ship)—the period of time when a person is learning a job by experience under a skilled worker

bacteria (bak-TEER-ee-uh)—a small living thing

chemical (KEH-muh-kuhl)—a substance that can cause a change in another substance

code (KOHD)—a set of laws

fixture (FIKS-cher)—something that is fixed or attached to a building

hazmat (HAZ-mat)—a material that would be dangerous to life or to the environment

install (in-STAWL)—to make something ready to be used in a certain place

respirator (RES-puh-rey-ter)—a device worn over a person's mouth and nose so that they can breathe

septic tank (SEP-tik TANGK)—a tank in which the solid matter of continuously flowing sewage is broken down by bacteria

LEARN MORE

BOOKS

Huddleston, Emma. *Plumbers on the Job.* Exploring Trade Jobs. Mankato, MN: The Child's World, 2020.

Mattern, Joanne. *Disgusting Jobs.* That's Disgusting! Minneapolis: Kaleidoscope, 2020.

Nickel, Scott. *World's Grossest Jobs.* Minneapolis: Lerner Publications, 2021.

WEBSITES

10 Ways You Can Help Save the Oceans
oceana.org/living-blue/10-ways-you-can-help-save-oceans

Sewage Treatment Facts for Kids
kids.kiddle.co/Sewage_treatment

Water Conservation Resources for Kids
wateruseitwisely.com/kids/

INDEX

GHOST SHIPS, ARE SHIPS REALLY HAUNTED?

BOLT